STEAM IN

EAST ANGLIA

First published 1980

ISBN 0 907087 01 9

BECKNELL BOOKS
P.O. BOX 21
KING'S LYNN
PE30 2QP

For October.

Designed by Becknell Studio

Printed in Great Britain by Galliard (Printers) Ltd, Great Yarmouth

STEAM IN
EAST ANGLIA

Colin Shewring

BECKNELL BOOKS
NORWICH AND KING'S LYNN

Contents

Introduction	5
Norfolk railway map	6
Norfolk	7
Norfolk steam	8
Cambridgeshire railway map	28
Cambridgeshire	29
Cambridgeshire steam	30
Suffolk railway map	50
Suffolk	51
Suffolk steam	52
Essex railway map	72
Essex	73
Essex steam	74
Tail lamp	94

Acknowledgements

I would like to acknowledge the help I have received in preparing this book from the following: M. E. Back, Mrs N. Back, E. Blakey, the staff of Galliard (Printers) Ltd, Great Yarmouth, GGS Photography, Norwich, I. E. Watson and A. C. Whittaker. To the photographers my thanks. The photographic credits are: Dr Ian C. Allen—1, 13, 14, 60, 62; late E. L. Back collection—63; R. W. Beaton, courtesy N. E. Stead—86; M. D. Beckett—146; A. E. Bennett—7, 18, 25, 42, 66, 68, 104, 119, 120, 138; R. C. Bishop—145; H. C. Casserley—36, 55, 71, 76, 87, 96, 122, 125, 129, 130, 131, 142; R. M. Casserley—143; R. E. Dean—2, 8, 20, 21, 29, 30, 31, 32, 35, 39, 51, 52, 69, 70; J. G. Dewing, courtesy N. E. Stead—50, 139; B. L. B. Fisher—147; T. G. Hepburn—6, 38, 40, 54, 56, 57, Front cover; H. N. James—37, 73, 74, 75, 77, 78, 79, 80, 81, 82, 83, 84, 85, 94, 97, 98, 99, 109, 110, 111, 113, 114, 115; O. G. Jarman—100; R. A. King—137; L&GRP collection, courtesy David & Charles—43, 64, 67, 89, 112; LCGB Ken Nunn collection—12, 49, 58, 59, 141; Locomotive Publishing Co.—44, 45, 65, 72, 133, 135; Dr W. J. Naunton—34, 95, 108, 116; D. C. Pearce—148, 149; Real Photographs Co. Ltd—9, 10, 11, 47, 88, 90, 93, 106, 117, 118, 121, 123, 126, 127, 132, 134, 136, Back cover; N. E. Stead—61, 144; late E. Tuddenham, courtesy M&GN Circle—19, 26; P. Waylett—46, 48, 103, 124, 128, 140; G. A. Yeomans—3, 4, 5, 15, 16, 17, 22, 23, 24, 27, 28, 33, 41, 53, 91, 92, 101, 102, 105, 107.

Front cover: 70013 Oliver Cromwell at Norwich Thorpe.
Back cover: F2 7112 and B12/3 61561 at Beccles.

Introduction

In compiling this selection of photographs illustrating steam at work under the wide skies of East Anglia, an author is faced not only with the problem of what to put in and what to leave out, but with the task of determining the extent of East Anglia. This latter has meant looking at the railway geography of the province, taking recent boundary changes into account and including broadly all the lines east of and including the Great Northern main line south of The Wash, excluding the Greater London area.

Steam was to be found in fascinating variety here, whether your choice was the Mid Suffolk or the Kelvedon & Tollesbury lines, the trams at Wisbech and Upwell or the alas unillustrated but much-loved narrow gauge Southwold Railway. You may prefer to remember the ageing 0-6-0s and 2-4-0s on the branch lines with their six-wheel coaches still running in the 1950s or the outer reaches of the Great Eastern's suburban network. But the cream of the LNER stock was to be found on the Great Northern main line, hauled by Gresley, Thompson and Peppercorn pacifics.

The most significant event for steam was probably the post-nationalisation selection of the Liverpool Street to Norwich route for the introduction of the very latest in steam traction, the beautiful 7MT *Britannia* pacifics. This first post-war inter-city service was so successful that it was eventually to be powered by the first BR main line diesels. So it was that the success of the *Britannias* in East Anglia was to be the harbinger of the first area of BR to be totally without steam.

Nothing today can compare with the power and beauty of the pre-diesel *Broadsman, East Anglian, Fenman* or *Hook Continental* expresses, but a taste of such delights is fortunately with us thanks to enthusiasts who have put care and effort into the preservation of much that was best in the steam world. There are a number of lines and steam centres in society ownership, but main line steam has not been seen very recently, though the author recalls occasional visits by *Flying Scotsman* and the Southern 4-6-0 *Greene King* and hopes to see them steaming on East Anglian main line metals again.

Until then, I hope this book will remind you of the pride of steam in East Anglia at the height of its achievements.

Colin Shewring
July 1980.

Norfolk railway map

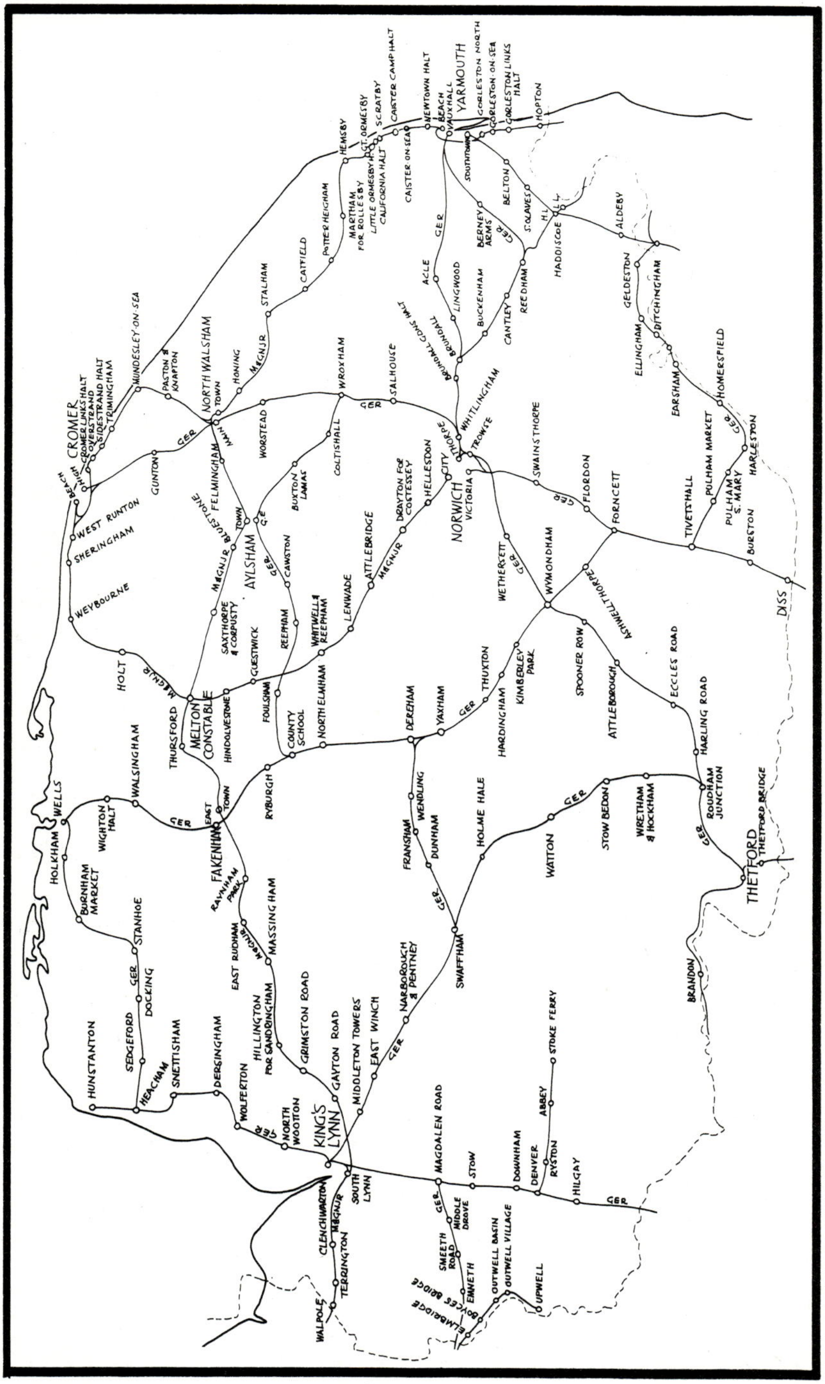

Norfolk

One hundred and twenty locomotives were allocated to Norwich Thorpe and its sub-sheds in 1953, giving some idea of the needs of the service network radiating from the city. The criss-crossing of branches was still hardly altered from GE days with great duplication. The Norwich to Liverpool Street trunk route was the original GE route which extended northwards as far as Cromer. This route (together with trains via Thetford as far as the Norwich services were concerned) remained largely undisturbed until the early 1950s.

The coming of the *Britannia* pacifics, after experiments with the Bulleid variety, revolutionised timings and the route became the fastest on the whole of BR whilst things got back to normal after the war. Soon the emphasis was put on the slightly shorter line via Diss and Ipswich.

Cromer High was closed in 1954 and trains were diverted to the Beach station, once the terminus of the rival M&GNJR. This latter line crossed Norfolk from east to west on its way from Yarmouth to the Midlands via King's Lynn. Every place of note on this route was served by both companies, because of the complexity of lines, with the exception of the M&GN works town Melton Constable and of Sheringham, to which the GE had running powers. Some rural sections, such as Heacham–Wells and Cromer–Mundesley, were so thinly trafficked that it was no surprise when BR closed these lines and others in 1953.

King's Lynn was an important centre, both on the M&GN line with its South Lynn major loco changing point and on the GE with its Hunstanton, Dereham and March branches. The Liverpool Street *Fenman* service mirrored the fast trains on the easterly London route with many creditable performances, especially when hauled by the 4-6-0 *Sandringhams*. These latter remind us of Wolferton station used by royalty from their nearby home.

Motive power, apart from a mixture of M&GN, Midland and later LMS types, was fairly typical of East Anglia in general. It varied from antique GE classes such as E4 2-4-0s and J15 or J17 0-6-0s, to *Claud Hamilton* 4-4-0s and B12 4-6-0s, to the Gresley LNER period typified by the B17 *Sandringhams*, to the Thompson B1 4-6-0s and L1 2-6-4Ts and to the very last word in steam, the *Britannia* 7MT pacifics. The latter were the apex of steam power and were loved by the GE men whose pride and joy they were—finest symbols of steam in East Anglia.

Norfolk steam

1. Norwich City, where J17 65559 is seen shunting, was the M&GN terminus. Bombed in the war, the station was rebuilt in a mean, prefabricated fashion.

2. Thompson B1 4-6-0 61050 waits to leave Norwich Thorpe, the city's main terminus, with the up *East Anglian* on 26th May 1951. The station dome is a well-known landmark.

3. Holden D16/3 4-4-0 62511 stands at No. 5 platform. This photograph illustrates the Gresley and the Thompson schools of thought regarding coach design.

4. BR standard but GE tradition: express headcode discs are displayed by *Britannia* 7MT pacific 70013 *Oliver Cromwell* at Thorpe in September 1956.

5. Thompson L1 2-6-4T 67714 departs Norwich on 11th July 1955 with a local for Lowestoft Central. Lowestoft was the tank's home shed at the time.

6. Another *Britannia*, 70001 *Lord Hurcomb*, draws into Norwich Thorpe in the early 1950s with the down *Norfolkman* under the extremely high GE lower quadrants.

7. North Walsham possessed both the M&GN Town station and the GE's more important-sounding Main. B12/3 4-6-0 61566 leaves North Walsham Main on 30th August 1958.

8. Heading northwards from Diss, Thompson B1 4-6-0 61233 hauls an express from Liverpool Street formed of BR standard Mark 1 bogies on 16th April 1955.

9. *Intermediate* E4 2-4-0 62787 stands at Tivetshall, junction for the Waveney Valley line, with a Norwich–Beccles train in April 1949. The horse boxes recall a bygone traffic.

10. Yarmouth South Town was the home depot of rebuilt *Gobbler* F5 2-4-2T 67199. It is seen at its home station on a Beccles all-stations local.

11. Vauxhall was the other GE terminus at Yarmouth. D16 4-4-0 62586 stands awaiting its load with a Norwich train. The Bure bridge can be seen behind the loco.

12. With the shunter riding the cab steps, J65 0-6-0T 8215, still in LNER livery on 1st September 1949, rumbles over the Bure bridge down towards Yarmouth's quays.

13. The M&GN terminated its mostly single-track main line at Yarmouth Beach, continuing to Lowestoft over the N&SJR. This view shows class C No. 4 leaving the terminus.

14. North of Yarmouth the Joint ran along the coastal sand dunes for some distance. Typical of M&GN power in the 1950s, Ivatt 4MT 2-6-0 43157 heads northwards.

15. At Cromer the M&GN had another Beach station, which was far more conveniently located than the rival GE establishment. B12/3 4-6-0 61547 has just arrived there from Norwich in September 1957.

16. Cromer High was strict GE territory. D16/3 4-4-0 62555 waits to depart with the 9.20 a.m. Sheringham–Norwich Thorpe in July 1954, two months before closure.

17. Ivatt 4MT 2-6-0 43145 eases tender first into Sheringham with the mid-afternoon Cromer Beach–Melton Constable local during the 1957 summer.

18. The M&GN's centre at Melton Constable is seen on the last day of through services—28th February 1959. 43145—again—arrives with the 12.56 p.m. ex Yarmouth.

19. Earlier that month, another Ivatt 4MT—43108—crosses the Ouse bridge at South Lynn with the 11.50 a.m. King's Lynn–Peterborough. The bridge was a holiday Saturday bottleneck.

20. King's Lynn, the Great Eastern terminus, housed a separate railway community. D15 62507 shunts coaches into the station, past a fine array of stock in the sidings.

21. A murky January 1951 day saw *Royal Claud* 62614 coming off the Hunstanton branch with the royal train. B2 61671 *Royal Sovereign* waits to take the train forward.

22. On 6th September 1957 N7 69619 stands at King's Lynn No. 3 with the 10.27 a.m. Hunstanton. C12 67386 at No. 5 heads the South Lynn push-pull.

23. The Holden J17 0-6-0s were rated 2P/4F, showing their true design purpose. 65582 of the class eases under Hunstanton footbridge on an unfitted freight.

24. Pulling over to the down platform passing loop, a *Claud Hamilton* D16/3 4-4-0 enters Heacham with a Hunstanton train. The month is holiday July in 1953.

25. Burnham Market, where Cambridge's E4 2-4-0 62785 is seen on 12th July 1959 on a special working, was the only place of any size on the Heacham–Wells line.

26. The 4.20 p.m. Dereham–Wells headed by D16/3 4-4-0 62540 passes J17 0-6-0 65537 with a Wells–Dereham freight at Fakenham East on 24th July 1955.

27. Dereham was subjected to inspection in July 1955 for J15 0-6-0 65471 was on a District Engineer's special when caught by the camera. The saloon is of Gresley origin.

28. There is a flurry of activity on the otherwise quiet platform at Swaffham as D16/3 62610 pauses in July 1955 with a Norwich–King's Lynn working.

29. B17/4 4-6-0 61672 *West Ham United*, one of the *Footballers*, roars through Harling Road with a summer express from the North. The use of discs lasted into diesel days.

30. Pacific power in the shape of 70005 *John Milton* leaves Thetford with the 8.24 a.m. Liverpool Street–Norwich on 28th July 1953. The tall signals indicate the bend.

31. On the same day, B17/6 4-6-0 61619 *Welbeck Abbey* stands at Thetford on a Peterborough East–Norwich parcels. The driver is obviously taking a breather.

32. 1953 was in the period before the Ipswich line became supreme. *Britannia* pacific 70010 *Owen Glendower* approaches Thetford on an up Liverpool Street express.

33. Deep in Norfolk's south-west corner was the agricultural Wissington Light Railway. *Wissington* pauses while a wagon is checked on the weighbridge on 6th September 1957.

34. Manning Wardle 0-6-0sT *Newcastle* of 1901 waits at Abbey on 24th October 1965. The GE Stoke Ferry branch platform, long in disuse, can be seen.

35. *Claud Hamilton* D16/3 4-4-0 62529 storms into Downham on 21st July 1956 with the Hunstanton portion of a down Liverpool Street express.

36. The Wisbech & Upwell Tramway ran for most of its length just inside the Norfolk boundary. 07125 and 07126 are surrounded by fruit baskets at Upwell on 25th June 1929.

Cambridgeshire railway map

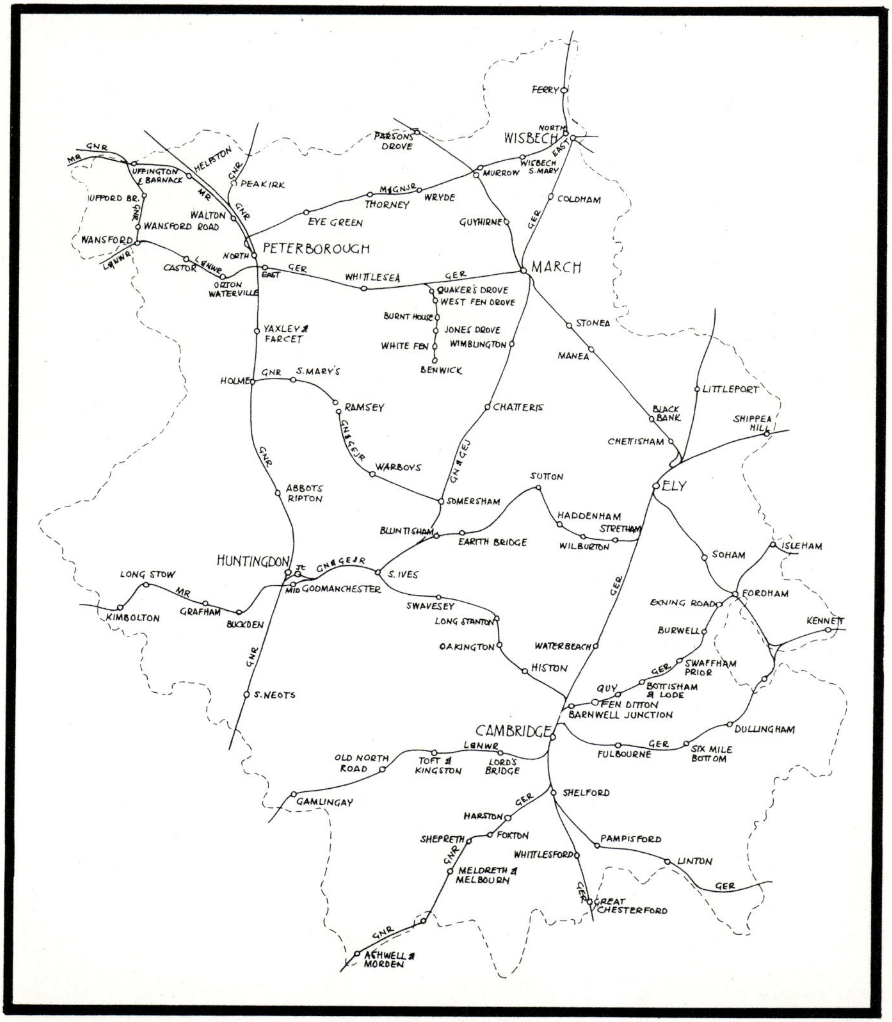

Cambridgeshire

Cambridgeshire (taking its modern boundaries) was the county of colour in steam days. The County Town saw the liveries of four companies, whilst Peterborough—though admittedly in Northamptonshire when steam still thundered down the Great Northern—boasted five: the apple green of the Great Northern itself, the red of the Midland, the golden gorse of the M&GN, the blackberry black of the LNWR and the dark blue of the Great Eastern.

Cambridgeshire remains the county of key points for access to the rest of the East Anglian rail network. The Midland from Leicester and the LNWR Rugby and Northampton lines met at Peterborough the Great Eastern and M&GN routes running into the area. All connected with the Great Northern London–Edinburgh East Coast Main Line. The M&GN crossed the GN & GE Joint route from the North at Murrow on its way to Wisbech (home of the famous Wisbech & Upwell Tramway, which ran mainly in Norfolk). The GN & GE Joint was a major freight route, March with its Whitemoor marshalling yards being the main access keypoint. From Peterborough the Great Eastern ran via Whittlesea and March to Ely. This was another crossroads, where the Norwich, King's Lynn, Bury St Edmunds and Cambridge routes, plus the meandering St Ives line, all met the route from Peterborough.

The M&GN never served Cambridge but the other four companies reached the University City. Though Cambridge was mainly Great Eastern (the Midland and the Great Northern had running powers over the Great Eastern) the LNWR *Premier Line* ran its Bletchley line on to Oxford, giving an academic flavour to this particularly interesting cross-country route. The Great Northern line, of course, competed with the Great Eastern route for undergraduates' and their mentors' fares to Town by running the *Cambridge Buffet Expresses*, known to the students as the *Beer Trains* because of the refreshment facilities on board!

Cambridgeshire steam

37. J15 0-6-0 65478 lurks inside Cambridge shed in October 1958. The tender cab was fitted for working the Colne Valley route to Marks Tey.

38. 65448 was allocated to Stratford when photographed leaving the south bay at Cambridge. The lower quadrant signals and Gresley stock lend age to the scene.

39. Cambridge had a fine array of electro-pneumatic signals. 61640 *Somerleyton Hall* stands at the down starters on 20th April 1954, having just arrived on a London relief.

40. The long platform at Cambridge is fitted for two-way working. B17/6 4-6-0 61638 *Melton Hall* stands at the south end with an up Liverpool Street express.

41. With safety valves lifting, J15 65438 waits in the bay at Cambridge with the Mildenhall branch train. *Blood and custard* coach livery was standard in 1955.

42. On 28th March 1959 Cambridge loco yard housed B2 4-6-0 61644 *Earlham Hall*, K3/2 2-6-0 61835 receiving attention, E4 2-4-0 62785 and others.

43. The LNWR at Cambridge is recalled by this 1938 view of LMS *Prince of Wales* 4-6-0 25845 leaving with a Bletchley train. Stirling No. 1 was on exhibition.

44. Gresley V3 2-6-2T 451 in austerity *NE* livery skirts Trumpington on a Cambridge–Liverpool Street working. The leading vehicles are a Quad-art set.

45. Austerity livery is also worn by streamlined A4 4-6-2 4484 *Falcon* seen during wartime—1943—on an empty coaching stock train near Shepreth.

46. The 4.1 p.m. Cambridge–Marks Tey makes a fine sight as it is smartly hauled by a typical Colne Valley route Ivatt 2MT 2-6-0. The train is near Pampisford.

47. The angular roof of Cambridge Loco looms over Gresley K3/2 2-6-0 61850 standing with a Peterborough fast. The scene is dated August 1959.

48. A Fenland scene in the late 1950s at the almost unpronounceable Quy with a tender cab-fitted J15 0-6-0 leaving on a Mildenhall–Cambridge all-stations train.

49. Another J15, 5350, shunts the 10.35 a.m. Cambridge–Mildenhall goods at Bottisham on 15th October 1949. The shunter is splitting the train some seven wagons back.

50. The Mildenhall branch crossed the Ely–Bury main line at Fordham. The station staff cycles up as E4 62785 blows off while waiting the right away.

51. *Claud Hamilton* D16/3 4-4-0 62529 approaches Ely on an up stopping train from March on 25th August 1952 past the three-way splitting distant.

52. On the same day, J15 0-6-0 65356 was photographed accelerating in the opposite direction with the rather short stopping pick-up goods to March.

53. Freight on the GN & GE Joint was very heavy—as evidenced by this view of a K3 2-6-0 at St Ives—for the line was a vital bypass to the trunk routes.

54. March was an excellent place for variety, many engine changes taking place there. K3/2 mogul 61826 picks its way through March station with a Yarmouth special.

55. Under March's superb GE arched station roof, D16/3 4-4-0 62589 stands on a local passenger on 25th August 1950. The *British Railways* tender legend dates the scene.

56. Another *Claud Hamilton* D16/3 4-4-0, 62570, with a badly marked smokebox stands in the bay platform at March with a three-coach local.

57. *Earlham Hall*, that is B17/6 61644 fitted with Westinghouse brake pump, makes a fine exhaust pulling out of March station with a short Saturday extra.

58. Rebuilt with Gresley large round top boiler, D16/3 62531 leaves Wisbech East on 28th August 1951 with the 2.15 p.m. King's Lynn–Cambridge via St Ives.

59. The disc headcode indicates a stopping passenger, in fact the 4.6 p.m. March–King's Lynn, seen leaving Wisbech East in the charge of D16/3 62569.

60. Wisbech North was the competing M&GN station. Ivatt 4MT 2-6-0 43142, seen from the windows of Horseshoe Lane box, sets off towards Peterborough.

61. *Claud Hamilton* D16/3 62567 of Cambridge pauses at Wisbech East. This view clearly shows the rather open appearance of the locos following removal of the slotted valences.

62. A WD 2-8-0 with two brake vans takes the M&GN route at the unique crossing with the GN & GE Joint located at Murrow. The cut-off spur is in the foreground.

63. Brick traffic was heavy around Peterborough. Eye Green on the M&GN main line is the location of this scene of an unidentified B1 4-6-0 shunting the brick works.

64. Kirtley 1P rebuild 2-4-0 137 of 1875 heads a Peterborough–Birmingham train out past Peter Brotherhood's works in early LMS days, circa 1926.

65. A1 pacific 60124 *Kenilworth* roars across Werrington troughs with the up *Flying Scotsman* in this April 1951 view. The fireman is clearly hard at work.

66. Peppercorn A1 pacific 60125 *Scottish Union* heads into Peterborough North with an up Pullman on 25th August 1962. 60125 was withdrawn two years later.

67. Robinson Great Central D9 4-4-0 6040 meets Holden Great Eastern J17 0-6-0 8208 by Peterborough East coaling stage. The D9s worked the M&GN for a few years.

68. WD *Austerity* consolidation 90239 clatters across the points at Crescent Junction, north of Peterborough North, with a freight on 2nd May 1959.

69. Abbots Ripton station still displays LNER advertisement boards on 14th April 1952 as A4 4-6-2 60030 *Golden Fleece* roars through on the up *Northumbrian.*

70. Almost a year before, on 24th March 1951, the same pacific accelerates through Huntingdon North station platforms with an up Leeds/Bradford express.

71. Crowds are a common sight on railtours today but somewhat unusual before the war. Stirling No. 1 takes water at Huntingdon on 11th September 1938.

72. Gresley V2 2-6-2 60903 is seen at St Neots on the down *Scotch Goods* in 1956. This class was named *Green Arrows* after the fast freight of that name.

Suffolk railway map

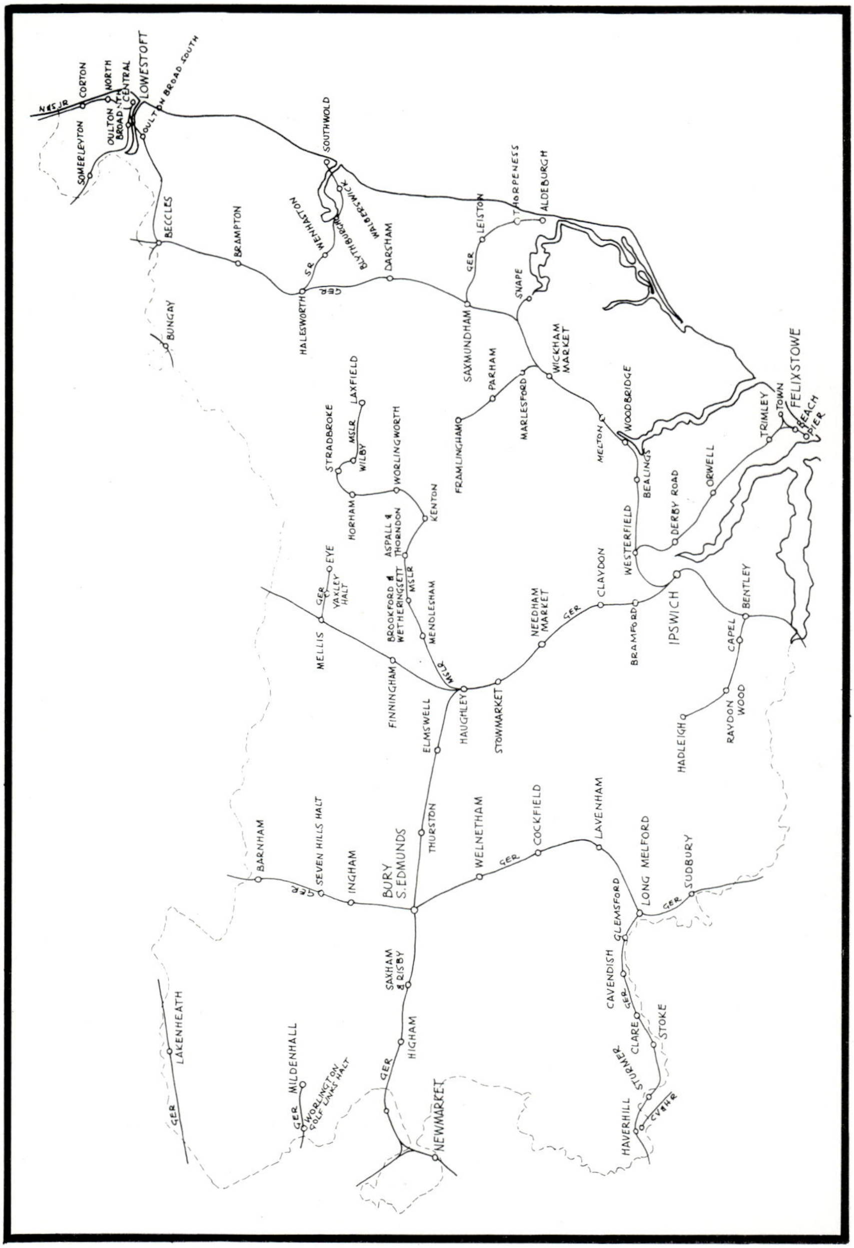

Suffolk

The Suffolk County Town of Ipswich was fascinating in steam days. The long row of station buildings, seemingly entering the dark tunnel at the southern end, fronted the departure platforms for the cross-country route via Bury St Edmunds to Cambridge and the North, the surprisingly switchback East Suffolk line to Lowestoft, the Felixstowe branch and the through main line from Norwich to Liverpool Street.

Ipswich had many of the crack workings before Stratford and Norwich monopolised the main line trains. The railwaymen of Suffolk turned out locomotives and stock in immaculate condition, GE-style cream painted cab roofs not being unknown. Water troughs were situated south of the locoshed and a *Britannia* taking water at speed was an impressive sight though it was hard work for the fireman operating the scoop. Quieter work was found on the Docks with tram locos and smaller tanks.

The Waveney Valley line came in at Beccles on the way to Lowestoft. The sleeper depot there was famous as the home of Sentinel shunters. It was also the southern terminus of the M&GNJR, whose golden gorse locomotives worked over the Norfolk & Suffolk Joint from Yarmouth until absorption by the LNER in 1936.

The Bury line branched off the Norwich line at Haughley, where the Mid Suffolk Light also came in. The Bury route was used by the Harwich–Manchester/Liverpool trains, notably the *North Country Continental* which was worked out and home by B12 4-6-0s or, in later years, by *Britannias*.

A long route from King's Lynn to Colchester was the original aim of early railway promoters with Bury as its centre. The lines were built but never worked as one but rather as a series of branches and the line through Long Melford and Sudbury was a favourite for seeing *Intermediate* E4 2-4-0s.

So too was the Mildenhall branch from Cambridge. The terminus was just inside the county of Suffolk and the line was famed for its eccentricity. Over the years it must have attracted hundreds of keen photographers. The last serving E4—the last 2-4-0 in regular use in the country—happily has been preserved in the National Railway Museum at York.

73. Derby Road is the other Ipswich station—on the Felixstowe branch. The L1 2-6-4Ts were a common sight on this line, this one storming over Spring Road viaduct.

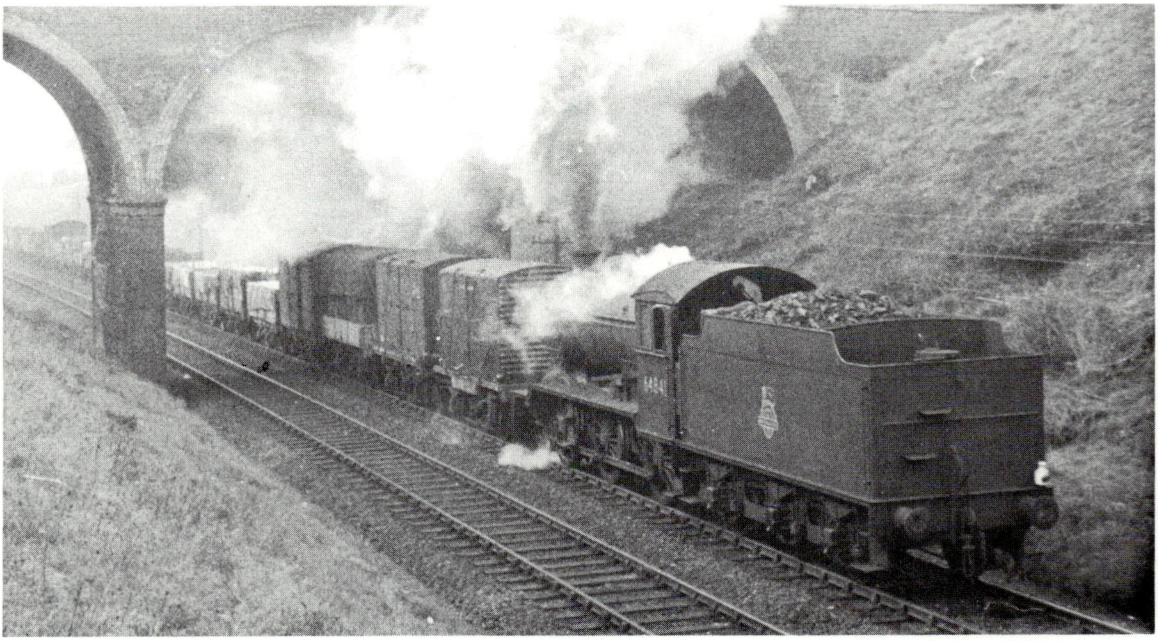

74. J39 0-6-0 64841 struggles tender first up the 1 in 90 to Westerfield with a mixed freight for Felixstowe dock on 10th March 1957.

75. The signalman waits ready with the tablet on 30th December 1958 as Thompson L1 2-6-4T 67706 brings the 2.1 p.m. Felixstowe Beach–Ipswich out of Felixstowe Town.

76. Although this industrial scene taken on 14th May 1956 belies the fact, Felixstowe Beach station on the line down to the dock was very close to the sea.

77. Coronation Year 1953 saw a special headboard as well as the usual *Broadsman* one on the front of *Britannia* 7MT 70007 *Coeur-de-Lion* leaving Ipswich.

78. The gantry at Ipswich boasted some fine signals, including GE calling-on arms. J39 0-6-0 64752 on a passenger passes B12 4-6-0 61557.

79. Ipswich station and tunnel can be seen in the background of this view of K2/2 2-6-0 61777, then allocated to Stratford, heading north on a down freight.

80. B17 61631 *Serlby Hall* waits on an up express at Ipswich platform, whilst sister loco 61625 *Raby Castle* passes non-stop on a holiday train.

81. Grimy J67/1 0-6-0T 68586 causes a traffic jam as it pulls its train over the level crossing at Stoke Bridge on the extensive Ipswich docks system.

82. *Battle of Britain* 4-6-2 34057 *Biggin Hill* stands on Ipswich turntable on 21st October 1951. The Southern locos were sent eastwards on loan before the *Britannias* arrived.

83. Towards the end of steam days, the *Britannias* were still on the express workings. On 18th March 1961 70010 *Owen Glendower* departs Ipswich with the 9.45 a.m. Liverpool Street.

84. Rural tranqillity at Framlingham, terminus of the branch from Wickham Market, which survived until 1965. F6 2-4-2T 67230 awaits departure.

85. The Snape branch was goods only. This classic shot of a J15 on a short freight running alongside the River Alde sums up its character well.

86. Saxmundham's staggered platforms can be seen—just—in this mid-1950s view of F6 2-4-2T 67220 pulling away gently with the Aldeburgh branch train.

87. Aldeburgh was noted for its overall roof, unusual for a GE branch terminus. J15 0-6-0 65447 was there with the Saxmundham train on 14th May 1956.

88. In LNER apple green livery and first style numbering, B12/3 4-6-0 8542 lifts a pre-war up Lowestoft express smartly past Beccles South signalbox.

89. Early BR days are recalled by this 1948 view of J15 0-6-0 65435 heading a freight tender first at Oulton Broad. Ten years on very little would have changed!

90. The Norfolk & Suffolk Joint route to Yarmouth was about to be traversed by F5 2-4-2T 67218 seen at Lowestoft Central in June 1954.

91. F5 2-4-2T 67187 takes on water while another of the class waits for departure time with the 2.36 p.m. Lowestoft Central–Norwich Thorpe.

92. Evidently due for a firebox rake-out is J15 0-6-0 65478 seen here dead on an outside road at Lowestoft shed in July 1955.

93. GE six-wheelers comprise the rake which *Gobbler* F4 7583 is hauling alongside Lake Lothing at Lowestoft. A shirt-sleeved p.w. gang works in the distance.

94. Lowestoft sleeper depot was famous for its Sentinel Y3 0-4-0T shunters. Departmental 40, formerly 68173, rumbles across the quayside crossover on 28th May 1960.

95. J17 0-6-0 65558 shunts the Co-op factory at Lowestoft. Bicycles are greatly in evidence, the flagman doubtless ready for a quick departure!

96. From Haughley the GE's only standard gauge competitor in Suffolk—the Mid Suffolk Light—ran 27 miles to Laxfield. 65447 shunts there on 1st September 1951.

97. The Mid Suffolk lived a peaceful life, crews being required to open and shut all gates. Trains were thus slow but closure didn't come until 1952.

98. The fireman and guard both look back as 65447 takes a stopping passenger, consisting of two Great Eastern vintage bogies, smartly out of Haughley.

99. Seventeen days before closure to goods of the Bury–Thetford line, J17 65589 passes Ingham on 10th June 1960. The passenger station was closed in 1953.

100. This 1873 view of Bury St Edmunds station shows its dignity and spaciousness, sadly now largely hidden. Waiting at the down starters is a GE *Little Sharpie* 2-4-0.

101. Coal wagons share Bury St Edmunds shed with engines in this September 1959 view. Nearest the camera are J17 0-6-0 65561 and an unidentified J15.

102. The simple coaling facility at *31E* can be seen close to—with its side door down—in this shot of sister J17 65502 dead on the pit.

103. N7 0-6-2T 69616 takes the 3.15 p.m. Long Melford–Bury St Edmunds three-coach local briskly towards Lavenham on 20th April 1957.

104. Bury St Edmunds station, noted for its towers, on 7th August 1959 saw J15 65457 blowing off as it starts off on its journey to Sudbury.

105. *Intermediate* E4 2-4-0 62789 departs from Long Melford. The single-line tablet can be seen above the back of the driver leaning out to see the right away.

106. Ivatt C12 4-4-2T 67367, then allocated to Bury, stands under the long footbridge at Long Melford in April 1956 with a train for its home town.

107. Haverhill, junction of the Colne Valley and Stour Valley lines, is the location of 62789 waiting departure with the 4.29 p.m. ex Marks Tey in this 1957 view.

108. Sister loco 62785 requires three men to turn her on Mildenhall turntable. The fireman, taking things easy, had lost his hat on the outward trip!

Essex railway map

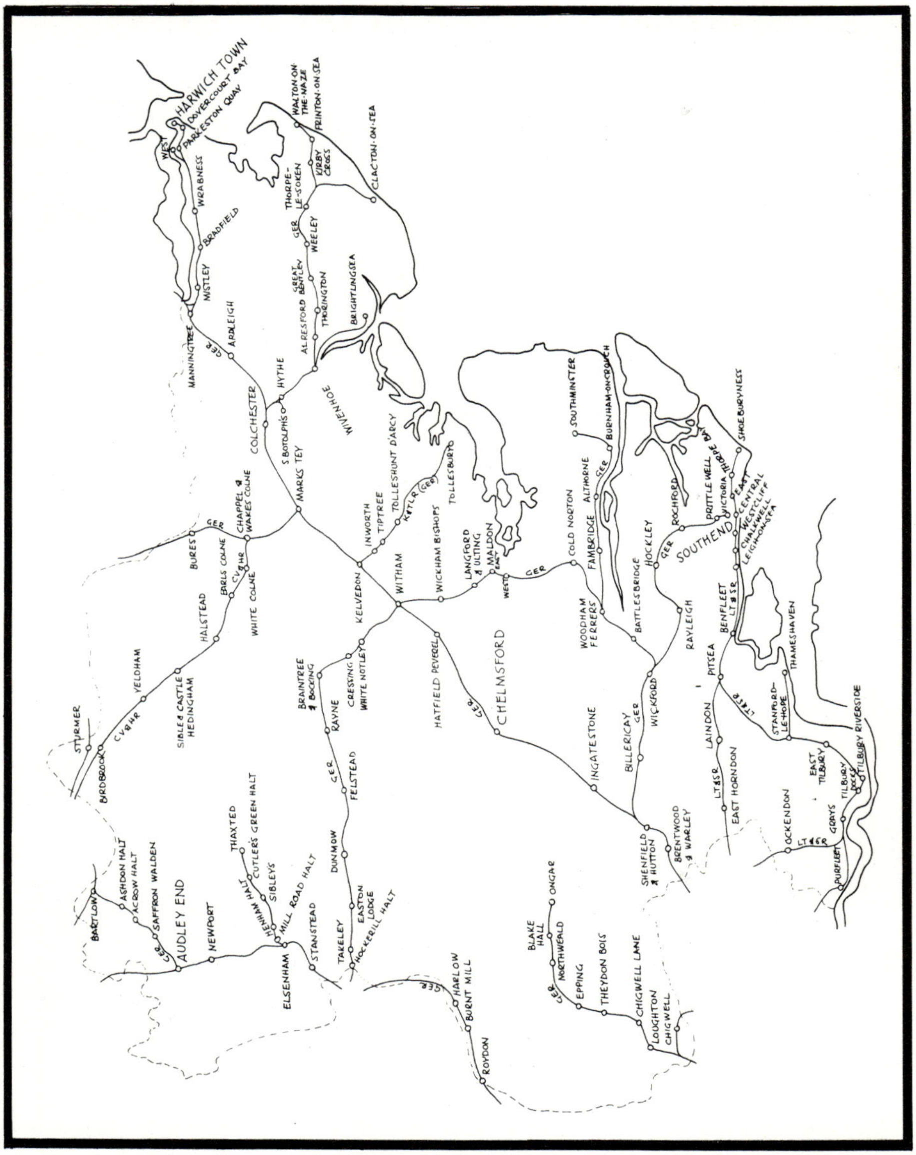

Essex

The railway geography of Essex is mainly that of the two Norwich–London main lines which run through the county and gradually converge as they near the Capital, together with cross-links and branches from the easternmost route to the coast. Continental traffic swells the Colchester main line services, being the result of the GE's development of Harwich as the premier port for the Low Countries.

Colchester was also the centre of a network which included the principal cross-country routes to Cambridge—the Stour Valley and the Colne Valley cut-off. The former at Chappel & Wakes Colne passed over the lengthy Chappel viaduct which was the Great Eastern's largest civil engineering feat.

The branch lines were the haunts of elderly E4 2-4-0s and J15 0-6-0s as well as the interesting LMS Ivatt 2MT 2-6-0s. Through holiday trains from the Midlands brought a wide variety of motive power to these lines and to their coastal destinations, principally Clacton. Electrification arrived early at Clacton and Walton, but in 1959 steam still held sway on the rest of East Anglia's railways. Three years later, steam as a motive power had practically disappeared.

The Midland Railway scored a point against the Great Eastern when it acquired the London Tilbury & Southend Railway under the nose of its rival. Although not East Anglia as generally defined, a little LMS variety along the north bank of the Thames enlivened the general scene. Southend, with its two terminii, included that of the GE where the commuter services were ably handled by the Holden B12 4-6-0s.

Audley End was a delight for the nostalgic. Here are the great tunnels with their decorative mouths designed in the style of the historic house at the insistence of the landowner. The Saffron Walden branch train would arrive, often a couple of Great Eastern bogies behind an ageing tank locomotive, and after making the connection would amble off down the branch as a *Sandringham* 4-6-0 plunged its gleaming rake of new *blood and custard* Mark 1 bogies in a plume of steam into the tunnel mouth. No moment of East Anglian steam was more impressive.

Essex steam

109. Worsdell J15 0-6-0s—the largest Great Eastern class built—were truly universal. This view of Colchester shows 65445 with sister 65466 moving up the yard.

110. 70036 *Boadicea* heads a rake of *blood and custard* liveried Mark 1 coaches southwards across the old layout at Colchester on 20th May 1955.

111. Colchester's face was to change drastically after electrification. It was steam, though, which worked the transformation: J19 64650 is seen on a 1961 electrification train.

112. Long before modernisation, E4 2790 in LNER livery stands with a clerestoried GE bogie on a local. This view of the old Colchester is dated June 1948.

113. 20th May 1956 was when J15 65475 pulled out of Colchester North with a similar train. By now the coaches were more modern Thompson stock.

114. The main Norwich–London line crossed the River Stour and the Essex/Suffolk border at Manningtree. B12/3 61523 takes the lengthy viaduct.

115. 70016 *Ariel,* before transfer to the WR, eases round the south curve at Manningtree with the Liverpool Street–Parkeston Quay *Day Continental* boat train.

116. Parkeston Quay shed in 1957 houses an unidentified J69 0-6-0T, N7/3 0-6-2T 69672 and J39 0-6-0 64777. The Derby Lightweight dmu is working from Manningtree.

117. Early BR days—April 1949—at Harwich Town. N7 0-6-2T 69614 stands at the platform, amidst empty stock in the sidings, with a Parkeston train.

118. A quiet Walton-on-the-Naze shelters suburban F6 2-4-2T 7220 laying over in April 1949. The clerestory coach is of interest as is the terminus' turntable.

119. The Clacton and Walton branches were electrified independently of the main system. Four months after energisation, 61057 takes the curve at Wivenhoe on 2nd August 1959.

120. Every schoolboy trainspotter's recollection of holidays is summed up by B1 61373 and D31 62069 simmering at the buffer stops at Clacton on 2nd August 1959.

121. A wonderful mixture of coaching stock of several pre-nationalisation periods comprises this up stopping train leaving Clacton behind D16/3 62549.

122. Tender-cabbed J15 65432 has run round its train at Brightlingsea on 7th July 1956 and is now being watered before returning to Colchester.

123. As an unidentified Ivatt 2MT 2-6-0 is attended to in the background, B2 4-6-0 61639 *Norwich City* eases round the curved branch platform at Marks Tey.

124. Another 2MT, 46465, has an easy job with the Colne Valley line afternoon freight, consisting of one open wagon and the brake van. The location is Birdbrook.

125. *Buckjumper* J69/1 0-6-0T 8636, the last of the class to be built, is seen on 26th June 1948 at Tiptree on the Kelvedon & Tollesbury Light Railway.

126. An Ipswich–Liverpool Street semi-fast slows into Witham behind B1 4-6-0 61005 *Bongo* in April 1949. One of the class nicknames was *Bongos*, from this loco.

127. 67192, one of the rebuilt F5 2-4-2Ts, stands at Braintree & Bocking with a two-coach train of Great Eastern vintage. The scene is dated April 1949.

128. The afternoon Maldon East–Witham freight, which includes some insulated containers, is hauled by J69/1 68579 along the single track branch on 28th February 1959.

129. Streamlined B17/5 2870 *City of London* climbs Brentwood bank on 15th July 1939, passing B12 8540 on a stopping passenger. The *LNER* colour light is noteworthy.

130. L1 2-6-4T E9011 shows a very early BR numbering style at Shenfield on 26th April 1948. The overhead is a reminder of LNER electrification progress.

131. Complete with the kitchen sink—A.C.F.I. water feed apparatus—and looking rather foreign, B12 8551 coasts past an interested motoring party near Billericay on 16th May 1936.

132. February 1955 and the fireman walks back along the platform to have a word with the guard as N7 0-6-2T 69630 waits at Southminster with a Wickford train.

133. LTSR 39 *Forest Gate* is seen head-on at Laindon with a Fenchurch Street train. The destination board and disc code are characteristic of the *Tilbury*.

134. B12/3 4-6-0 61557 pulls into Wickford with a Southend Victoria train in February 1955. Express passenger headlamps do not have the same appeal as GE discs.

135. The LTSR became an LMS outpost as this study of *Black Five* 4-6-0 5053 on a 1936 Southend Central–St Pancras train at Leigh-on-Sea amply demonstrates.

136. Double-headed LMS Stanier 2-6-4Ts 2506 and 2521 roar through the Essex countryside with a Southend Central–Fenchurch Street semi-fast.

137. Steam power of a different sort: Bagnall 2370 0-6-0 fireless of 1929 shunts across the public road at Proctor & Gamble's West Thurrock works on 2nd August 1977.

138. Squat West Ruislip-bound Central Line tube stock contrasts strangely with the familiar lines of F5 2-6-2T 67200 seen at Epping on 6th October 1957.

139. Before London Transport's electrification, Ongar was the terminus of just another quiet GE branch. 67203 sets off for Epping with the driver in a cheerful mood.

140. 67279 pulls into Ashdon Halt on 28th May 1956 with the 4.52 p.m. ex Audley End. This G5 0-4-4T was of Worsdell North Eastern design, introduced a few years after he left the GE.

141. The 4.25 p.m. Elsenham–Thaxted awaits departure at Elsenham on 22nd April 1935 with F5 2-4-2T 7193 in charge. This light railway closed in 1953.

142. Audley End is seen on 30th June 1951 as Thompson L1 2-6-4T 67723 brakes a Liverpool Street–Cambridge semi-fast into the down platform.

143. A peaceful summer's day is scarcely disturbed as regular engine G5 0-4-4T 67279 rambles between Audley End and Saffron Walden on 7th July 1956.

144. Suburban tank power at Saffron Walden as N7/2 0-6-2T 69692 of Cambridge arrives with the branch train from Audley End. Old rails support the wooden nameboard.

Tail lamp

145. Castle Hedingham is now the home of the Colne Valley Railway. Hunslet 0-6-0ST WD 190 is seen in steam there on the Easter 1977 Open Day.

146. Brighton-built standard 4MT 2-6-4T 80151 stands at Chappel on the Stour Valley Railway awaiting its next duty. Alas, full restoration is needed.

147. The North Norfolk Railway preserves two miles of the M&GN. On 12th March 1979 Peckett 0-6-0ST 5 *John D. Hammer* starts away from Sheringham.

148. LMS 2-6-4T 2500 seen at Bressingham. Built for the *Tilbury*, this loco was withdrawn from Shoeburyness shed in 1962 and came to Norfolk six years later.

149. Southern S15 4-6-0 841 *Greene King*, now on the NYMR, heads the lengthy 1977 Nene Valley Railway *Santa Special* past the Midland pattern signalbox at Orton Mere.